The AUSTRALIAN Women's ~~V~~ ~~s~~

Vancouver - Arlington, Nave

101 Glorious gardening ideas

By Fleur Kreel

Every gardener is drawn to pretty plants but plants alone won't make a lovely garden. It's where you put the plants, how you group them and what other accessories, features or structures you use that count. You'll see what we mean as you read this inspirational book. You'll see how dozens of other gardeners have made their gardens beautiful and memorable by planning and creating pretty scenes within them. And you'll find out how to adapt their ideas to suit your garden.

GARDENING EDITOR

❖ ❖ ❖

GROWING PRETTY PICTURES 2
VIEWS & VISTAS 5
FUSS FREE GARDENS 15
MASS PLANTING 23
TREE TRUNKS 29
SPOT COLOUR 34
FORMAL GARDENS 39
SHADY PLACES 44
ROMANTIC VISIONS 55
RARE OPPORTUNITIES 61
COLOUR SCHEMES 65

PATHS & STEPS 71
FLOWERING FRONTAGES 77
WALLS & SCREENS 85
BACKGROUNDS 89
GARDEN PICTURES 95
PLANTS & STONE 101
SIMPLE STRUCTURES 106
GARDEN PATTERNS 111
SMALL SPACES 116
VEGETABLES & HERBS 123
INDEX 128

Growing Pretty Pictures

*B*eautiful gardens don't just happen. They are planned long before a shovel is picked up or a plant purchased.

❧

Such planning starts with pretty ideas – a single idea or a collection of smaller ones that are attractive by themselves and stunning when arranged together.

❧

We've selected pictures filled with ideas to stimulate your imagination and inspire you. Whether it be for your entire garden or one small part of it, whether you are starting from scratch or renovating a troublesome corner. And it doesn't stop there!

❧

Captions, text and handy hints will help you to interpret the pictures, explain the ideas, and devise ways to make them work in your own garden.

❧

This book is not a formula or a prescription for a pretty garden, rather it is a starting point. Use it as

It is not these trees and flowers that make the scene, it's their arrangement into a pleasing view. You may live in a warm climate and not be able to use these plants but you can still use the design principles.

Ground covers boldly massed in undulating curves create a beautiful effect. A simple, broad-scale planting of drought-tolerant plants is a good idea for people who want pleasant surroundings that are easy to maintain.

a source of new ideas or of familiar ideas used in new ways.

❧

While we identify plants where possible, this is not a dictionary of plants. And while plants are specific to the conditions and climate of a certain locality, you need not be restricted to the plants shown in a picture to use that idea.

❧

Flowers at the front gate create a warm welcome. Envisaging the entrance to your home is a pleasurable and creative way to settle on the look you want for your garden.

Rather than copying the exact planting, our captions and text are intended to help you see how the plants shown have been used to create an effect. You could easily choose other plants to achieve a similar or better effect in your own garden. For instance, the idea shown may depend on low-growing, long-flowering perennials or tall, slim-trunked trees; perhaps its success is due to the use of warm, bright colours or a mix of boldly shaped, strongly textured leaves; maybe it's just the use of unusual accent plants or a harmonious mix of shrubbery. These are effects which can be mimicked by many different plants all over the world, not just the ones shown.

❧

Dainty spring flowers (Geum and Nigella) catch the eye with their vibrant, joyous colours. Primary colours mixed with white always look cheerful and bright. You can plan the timing and combinations of flower colours to bring beauty and pleasure to your garden at different times of the year.

Inside, you'll glean some of the practical, pretty and fundamental concepts of garden design. These include how to enhance distance in large gardens and create a feeling of space in smaller areas; ways to use flower and leaf colour to create effects in your garden; and how to arrange garden beds, paths, steps and ornaments in pretty ways to create everything from long vistas to small scenes.

❧

Sheltered and very shaded, this dim, cool spot is an eye-catching image of spring with its rock pool, woodland ferns and flowers. You could recreate this scene with dozens of other plants.

With these lovely pictures, it is easier to imagine your future garden and mentally arrange it as many times as you wish with little effort and no expense. You'll soon develop a clear vision of what it is that you want and how to go about making it a reality.

Views & Vistas

From lovely, long views seen through a framework of foliage to the charming, more intimate scenes, vistas and vignettes are so important in a garden. They give a garden a sense of space and structure and make investigating it a pleasure.

Everywhere you look there should be sights to see, pretty garden pictures to behold.

The spacious gardens presented here not only show what can be done on relatively grand scales, they give you ideas to be adapted for small spaces.

Make an entrance

You may have a long, hot walk to your front door so make it cool, gracious and inviting with a creeper-covered walk. If you have a dull, narrow passageway at the side of your house, you can make it appear broader and brighter with a painted pergola laden with flowers. The trip to the back garden then becomes a pleasant stroll instead of a featureless walk.

If your home is at the end of a long climb, you can make it an enjoyable experience with the sight and sound of water along the way. Alternatively, you could line both sides of your steps with a mixture of plants that are fragrant during the different seasons.

Gardens with a view

You can create interest and beauty in your garden with a woodland theme, such as that used in the view through the trees on page 8. Trees and plant combinations can enlarge the sense of space within a garden. They provide a frame through which to view a beautiful garden feature, such as a striking plant or ornament, or form a partial screen, allowing exciting glimpses of a feature through its foliage. We show you an intimate scene created around a statue on page 10, explain how to create views, and present some wonderful ways to use water, including pools, falls and fountains.

There are as many ways to create beautiful views within your garden as you care to imagine. Use these pictures to stimulate your imagination; you'll soon be dreaming up your own views.

Woodland walk

In this forest garden the path allows a long view before it disappears from sight. The gardener has made the most of the view by planting shade-loving plants such as Justicia, Hosta and a mixture of ferns. In a cooler climate local woodland plants would work as well.

PERGOLAS AND PAVILIONS

There is no more delightful way to create interest in a large garden than with structures such as arches, pavilions and pergolas.

When planning a walk or pavilion think about where to put it; not in the middle of an empty lawn where there is no reason for it. Such features need a pleasant purpose to make them work.

Whether freestanding or built against the house, an archway, pergola or pavilion can transport you from indoors to outdoors. It links different areas of the house and garden.

In the picture at right, Laburnum flowers fall between the widely spaced, supporting arches of the walkway while the end of the tunnel frames an intriguing glimpse of the garden beyond.

The climber you plant to cover a pergola could be any plant with pendulous flowers: *Wisteria sinensis, Datura suaveolens* and *Thunbergia mysorensis* are just three possibilites. Strictly speaking, Datura is a flexible shrub, not a climber, but then so is Laburnum.

Notice in this picture how the simple and consistent border of Erigeron accentuates the formal line of the path while remaining soft and pretty. It is just the right height and width to give the base of the arched pergola an impression of weight and solidity, an anchor to the ground. This is a desirable feature, particularly as these arches do not have a constructed foundation such as a masonry base.

For an even softer mood, consider the effect if the low daisy border were a succession of pastel coloured perennials in purples, blues, white, silver and cream, and of gently varied heights. Examples of flowers to use in such a border include foxgloves, Aquilegias, Gypsophila, Thalictrum, forget-me-nots and Lamium.

Proportion and scale are important to achieve the best effect from any garden feature. This means ensuring that the size and type of pergola or walkway is in keeping with the proportions and style of your home. The materials used should also suit. For instance, seen against buildings of brick or stone, solid pillars of masonry (cement or brick) with lighter timber beams may be appropriate. In a modern setting, dressed timber, machine-sawn timber or styled metal posts may be best.

Do not build your structure too high for its width and always make the posts relatively thick for the rafters they support. This will prevent your construction from looking gaunt and ugly.

Tunnel of flowers

A walk beneath this golden canopy on the petal-strewn path leads you towards the house and sunny lawn which is glimpsed through the gate. The pretty tunnel of Laburnum screens the eye from all side views and distractions and wraps your way in foliage and flowers in spring. It provides shade in summer and a tracery of stems in winter.

FRAMES AND BORDERS

Laburnum is a deciduous shrub or small tree that can be trained over a frame to form an arch. Its golden-yellow flowers are magnificent in spring. It is only successful where winter nights are always frosty and the days cool to cold. In warmer climates you could use Wisteria and, in subtropical areas, try a vine such as **Thunbergia mysorensis** *for a similar effect.*

The border planting is fleabane (**Erigeron karvinskianus**), *a spreading, low daisy that is suited to both cool and frost-free gardens. It flowers throughout the warmer months, almost year-round in a warm climate.*

SMALL GARDEN OPTION

Pergolas in small city courtyards and tiny spaces often require more slender posts and lightweight rafters. Keep the proportions of such pergolas in balance, that is, thicker and wider posts than rafters. Remember, too, lightweight structures will not support heavyweight plants, such as Wisteria.

View through the trees

In this enchanting woodland scene, silver birches (*Betula pendula*) frame the view with their upright slender trunks. The sunny flowers of Chinese cabbage in the foreground draw your eye to and through the vista, over the contrasting purple shades of the cinerarias to another splash of yellow, this time from a Laburnum in the mist. The bright colours and soft foliage create a light and airy mood, touched with the mystery of unexplored secrets.

WOODLAND FANTASIES

A woodland glade can be created almost anywhere in your garden. Its appeal is its informal arrangement of trees, just as they would occur in the wild.

In a large garden, a choice of any woodland tree amenable to planting in clusters would suit such a garden style. As well as the silver birch of cool climates, you could try *Populus tremula, Angophora costata, Eucalyptus maculata, Ceratopetalum apetalum* and *Doryphora sassafras*. Some of these, such as the Eucalyptus and the Angophora, grow to immense proportions in height and trunk girth in good soil and as single specimens. But in poorer conditions, or multi-planted where they compete with each other, such trees can create an enchanting glade.

Plant compositions that work

Enlarge the sense of space in your garden by placing trees, soft shrubbery and flowers between your garden and an open outlook.

Consider the plant composition in the garden at left; notice how the soft masses of green shrubbery fill the space between the birch trunks and the ground. This makes the trees look as if they belong. The greenery is also necessary to soften the flower colours, weaving them together in a harmonious tapestry.

The middle-ground plantings of cineraria in deep tones of purple and pink accentuate the shade beneath the trees. This shadow contrasts with the foreground brightness and the distant lightness, increasing depth and adding a sense of mystery.

Trees add depth

Also notice the effect of having one solid tree trunk and the lighter, but as emphatic, cluster of three slimmer trunks nearby. This accentuates depth and keeps the mood informal whereas a pair of trees, one either side of the view, would seem flat and unnatural in this setting.

In this garden composition the space looks deeper than if it were devoid of the tree trunk frame and you could see straight into the clearing beyond. And it looks larger than if it were screened off from the outlook by a hedge or fence. It is an interesting view because seeing things in glimpses, rather than all at once, excites our curiosity about what lies beyond.

You too can create interest and beauty in your garden with a woodland theme.

CONTINUING THE FANTASY IN THE CITY

The woodland scene pictured at left has been created in a big country garden, but it would suit a good-sized city garden.

Imagine the front fence where the birch trees are with a gate between them. If the gate led to a park, neighbouring garden or tree-lined street, it would create the impression of a garden that continued beyond your boundaries.

In a garden with a lesser outlook, try planting the woodland trees more thickly along your boundary. The garden would retain its woodland theme and such a dense array of trunks would screen out everything you did not wish to see. For this to be successful the screen of trees has to be deep – at least 3m (10ft) and preferably 4m (13ft).

CREATING A VIEW

Have a sight to see. This may be a favourite statue or seat, a vase on a plinth, a fountain, pond or just space to view the ever-changing sky or distant rooftops.

Create a frame to look through, using, say, a group of tree trunks, the interlacing boughs of a tree, an arc of an arbour, the space in a hedge or the silhouette of a pair of urns. The frame creates an illusion of depth and focuses your attention on the view by defining an edge around it.

Decide on the spot from which to look at a view. The view is unlikely to be successful from all directions. Try to create it where you will see it most often or where it invites the viewer to it, using steps, pathways or an open lawn.

With distance, objects appear smaller, colours paler and shape is less defined. Over smaller distances mimic this effect by using bright, primary colours and clear shapes in the foreground. Use pastel, muted colours and hazy shapes for the background.

Dark evergreens with large leaves appear to loom in on you; they narrow and enclose the view. Use hedges of yew (*Taxus baccata*) and conifers (*Cupressus torulosa*) or plant shrubberies of *Viburnum odoratissimum*, *Prunus laurocerasus* and *Camellia japonica* – all plants with smaller leaves.

Small-leafed plants can make a small space seem larger. *Buxus sempervirens* and *Buxus microphylla* 'Japonica', *Camellia sasanqua* and *Murraya paniculata* are good examples.

Foliage colour, texture and form are as important as flower colour in a gardener's palette. The silver *Helichrysum petiolaris*, the golden *Heliotropium arborescens* 'Aurea', the purple *Strobilanthes anethifolius*, the apple-green *Plumbago auriculata* are just some plants with pretty foliage that are worth remembering.

GO WITH THE FLOW

Whenever you have an idea, be bold in its execution. In the picture at left the composition could be made more dramatic if the statue were twice the width. A thicker ornament would make a stronger contrast with the slender tree trunks. The vertical theme would remain as strong but the tree trunks, appearing slimmer, would seem to recede, giving the scene a feeling of more depth.

You could make a different garden picture by contrasting the vertical elements with a cloud of flowers, such as Gypsophilas or Gauras, and a seat or a birdbath instead of a statue. In fact later on in the season in this garden, the flowers that succeed the foxgloves, do just that.

Make this scene an entire garden

This scene is part of a bigger garden but it could be a small garden on its own. Imagine a fenceline just beyond the group of trees and boundaries either side of the picture. This would provide enough space to support a miniature woodland garden and a seat to view it.

Vertical hold

In spring the pastel spires of foxglove flowers echo the ghostly, upright trunks of the silver birch and surround the owl ornament with make-believe forest. The owners of this garden have accentuated the verticality of the statue by surrounding it with other vertical elements – the slender tree trunks and the tall foxglove flower spikes.

SMALL GARDEN OPTION

When creating a woodland or placing any tree in a small garden, choose from the many small trees available. A tree with an extensive canopy and root system and large trunk diameter may damage underground pipes and overhead wires and push over boundary or retaining walls. It will also look out of scale with your house and garden.

A PLACE FOR A POOL

Water – cool, reflective and sparkling. Catch the light in transparent droplets of a fountain; catch the breeze as it ripples the still surface of your pool; watch petals and leaves float and fish swim; drown out the sound of traffic with the tinkling of a fountain or the splashing of a waterfall.

Ways with water

The best place for a pool or lake is in a natural depression, swampy ground or a spot that collects water after heavy rain. There may be a natural watercourse in your garden which can be dammed to make a lake as shown above, or shaped to make a stream.

It may already be a stream and only require fine tuning with a bridge or stepping stones, some rocks or boulders and new plantings such as water-loving trees, water Iris, ferns, bullrushes and sedges.

If you do not have a low-lying place that naturally suggests a pool, mound and shape your garden to create one. Excavated soil can be used to make the banks or you can nestle your pool amongst shrubbery.

There are endless shapes that a natural pool can take. Formal pools come in regular shapes such as rectangular, L-shaped, oval or round and look best when placed on level ground in the middle of lawn or paving. They may be enhanced with an attractive edge or blended into your garden scheme with planting on two or three sides.

To provide a reflection, pools must be dark. No more than a third of the surface should be taken up with waterlilies and other aquatic plants or you will lose sight of the water and your pool will look like another garden bed.

If you do not need access all the way around your swimming pool, try planting along one or two sides, partially enclosing it and blending it in with the garden. You may want to position a fountain in or near it or place large tubs of plants, a statue or an urn or two beside the pool. A small water plant such as duckweed can then be planted within your fountain or urn.

Falls and fountains

Waterfalls are wonderful features in a garden built on many levels. They can be built into terraces, steeply sloping ground or beside steps.

Fountains can be freestanding or part of a pool. Place where the jet can catch the light and you can hear the sound of the falling water. If you live on a busy street, a splashing, tinkling fountain cleverly masks the traffic noise.

Water can provide one grand scene within a garden or it can be an enticing or secret part of it – a narrow, meandering stream which surprises you when you see it between the shrubbery or beneath trees.

◄ Natural lake

The success of this vista lies in the generous size of the pool, a pool from which the garden is watered. Its undulating edge is obscured with planting. This, and the reflections in the tranquil surface, makes the space appear much larger than it is. A tapering lawn leads the eye to the pool. The light framework of trees and fence on the far bank separates the pool from its surroundings and provides glimpses of more garden beyond.

Formal setting ►

In a formal garden, a series of stone terraces, the fountain and clipped shrubberies gently lead the eye to the flower gardens and an arbour closer to the house. The translucent play of water, and the shimmer where it falls, contrast with the dark backdrop of the pool and its surrounds. The purple mass of two maples (*Acer palmatum* 'Atropurpureum') cleverly screens the beautiful vista beyond, heightening anticipation.

Fuss Free Gardens

Almost everyone wants to have a garden that is easy to maintain. We dream of never having to weed the beds or mow the lawn; never having to water, prune and tidy, feed and nurture with fertilisers or spray for pests. We just want to sit in the shade of the garden when we have the time to and enjoy it, or wander through it to pluck a few blossoms for display in a vase. Sadly, that dream is about as likely as the self-making bed or the no-clean bathroom. It's a fact that all gardens need regular maintenance.

It's also a fact that some gardens require much less care than others and all gardens can be made easier to maintain. Here we unravel the secret of the low maintenance garden.

Asking questions

In an easy care garden most of the work is done before the garden is planted. This involves learning as much as possible about your garden.

What's the climate like? Does it rain mostly in winter, summer, evenly throughout the year or hardly at all? What are the lowest and highest temperatures you can expect? Plants evolve around a specific range of temperatures. All have a minimum temperature they can survive and there are plenty that won't live through the heat of hot summers.

What's your soil like? Is it deep and rich or shallow and rocky? Perhaps it's heavy clay or thin sand, well-drained or boggy, acidic or alkaline. There are many variations and, as your garden has to live in the soil, it's important to know what the soil is like.

What about your garden's aspect? How sunny or shady the garden is will also influence the type of plants you can grow. The patterns of sun and shade change throughout the day and the year as the sun's angle in the sky changes. If you or your neighbour have deciduous trees, this will also influence the shade patterns throughout the year.

Know your needs

When you've worked out these basics, consider your own requirements. Do you want a lawn area on which children can play? Do you need a big space for entertaining or a small shady space for sitting? Do you want a "view" garden with features visible from inside the house? Be honest with yourself about how much time you will spend gardening.

If you take these factors into consideration and choose plants that will suit your site, you'll be well on the way to having a low maintenance garden.

Delightful repetition

This delightfully simple scene relies on one plant – lavender – repeated. Lavender works in this garden's climate so a lot of it has been used, massed along the edges of the paths and given plenty of space. The gravel path leads the eye gently to a group of *Eucalyptus citriodora*. The fine beauty of the tree trunks belies their drought hardiness but in cooler climates a trio of any slender trunked trees would suffice. There is not much maintenance to do here, apart from occasional raking of the gravel and annual pruning of the lavender and Artemis in winter.

Rodney Hyett

MAKING LIFE EASY

Surprisingly, beds containing trees, shrubs and flowers often require less work than lawn and are much more interesting. Another alternative to lawn is a paved area or deck for entertaining or for sitting and enjoying your garden. This requires little maintenance and it is a more practical surface for tables and chairs. If you like the soft feel or look of lawn, you may decide to keep it but there's often no need for acres of the stuff.

In an easy care garden you can fill spaces other than lawn, paving and paths with plants. Other features, such as ponds, arbours and potted plants, do not suit the easy garden style as they require extra work.

Space for trees

Where there is room for them, trees give a lot for very little effort. They create a lovely effect at a minimal expense and demand little in the way of maintenance. Keep in mind the size to which a particular tree will grow and its maintenance needs, such as pruning, watering and fertilising. Add some shrubs or flowers and you can have an enchanting garden that requires little effort.

Easy choice

This garden is designed to be looked at from the house above. It is composed very simply on a grid pattern and contains only five types of plant. A single Japanese maple (*Acer palmatum*) is centrally located amid squares of the tufty and slow growing ground cover, mondo grass (*Ophiopogon japonicus*). Contrasted with this is the grey-leaved lamb's ears (*Stachys byzantina*). There is also a cross of *Ajuga reptans* and some of the grids are cornered with the low ground cover, *Cotoneaster dammeri*.

MONDO MAINTENANCE

Over time the mondo grass will grow over the stepping stones and many gardeners would clip it, creating a stark, vertical wall of foliage. Avoid making this kind of regular work for yourself by removing the row along the edge of the path when it starts to encroach on the stones. Mondo grass grows slowly so this won't be a frequent chore (much less frequent than clipping) and you won't destroy the beauty of the design and this plant.

Designer: Matthew Taylor

Designer: Isabelle Greene

COASTAL FLOWERS

The plants shown in the picture at right are mostly daisy varieties, including **Chrysanthemum frutescens, Osteospermum ecklonis, Euryops pectinatus,** *and Gazania. There are also geraniums, alyssum, perennial wallflowers and some Iris. All are suited to the coastal conditions and accept the region's climate.*

Colourful daisies ▶

This hillside garden tumbling with flowers belongs to a holiday house. The owners are only here at holiday times (and some weekends) and when they do arrive they don't want to spend all their time caring for the garden. This colourful scene is the result of a simple and clever planting scheme. It consists almost entirely of daisy bushes in soft, rainbow colours. These plants by nature like the shallow rocky soil and full exposure to the sun.

◀ Thriving on neglect

Massed plantings of succulents and other drought tolerant plants flow in undulating curves in this beautiful garden of another holiday home. Large drifts of common iceplant or pigface make up the bulk of the planting with beds of bright orange Gazania, clumps of statice and swathes of succulent Sedum for variety and contrast. This is a spring garden, designed to be in bloom when the owners use their holiday home. For the rest of the year it has to look after itself, no easy task through this region's hot, very dry summer. However, this garden manages beautifully thanks to sensible plant selection.

WORK NOW, PLAY LATER

On many sites some preparative steps need to be taken before the planting can begin and your easy care garden is completed. If you are dealing with inhospitable areas of compacted soil or subsoil unearthed by previous building works, you may need to improve the soil. You can minimise these preparations by choosing plants appropriate to the main feature of the existing soil. For instance, you will never convert a clay soil into a sandy one, so don't try; grow plants that like clay soils instead.

It is not a low maintenance or desirable solution to excavate a chalky hillside and refill it with rich, acidic soil so that you can plant azaleas and Rhododendrons. What you can do is improve the existing soil with regular applications of compost or well-rotted manure. Even chalky soil will remain fairly alkaline but it will be more fertile and therefore able to sustain a wider range of lime-loving plants.

You may wish to install a properly designed irrigation system to supplement existing rainfall. In this case, ensure that water is not wasted by inaccurate sprinkler heads spraying onto paving or by run off from spray that is too fast for the rate of absorption (particularly on slopes). Do not water too often and, if you live in a dry climate, don't try to grow a rainforest.

Just one plant ▶

In a given space the more types of plants you grow, the more you have to know and do. Mass planting with one species makes for less work and can look better than a riot of colour. Here in a bed cut into a lawn, grey-leafed Gazanias flower virtually all year on just the run-off from the lawn sprinklers.

Designer: Raymond Hansen

STYLED FOR SUCCESS

You can create hard work or make it easy for yourself when you choose a style you'd like for the garden. Formal gardens that rely on clipped hedges and crisp, straight lawn edges demand a lot of time, as do gardens with masses of annual flowers or potted plants.

The easiest gardens to maintain are those with simple plantings of species that suit the climate and site (as in the picture at right) or those that take their lead from nature. This natural, very informal style of garden is allowed a degree of unkemptness. Its owners appreciate the natural beauty of fallen twigs, leaves and petals. Plants are allowed to spill over paths or self-sow in other parts of the garden.

Whichever style you choose, if you select plants that suit your climate and soil you will be rewarded with a beautiful, thriving garden. If you plant them simply, in groups and massed, and give them the room they need, you won't have to buy as many plants in the first place and you won't have to prune. Then if you want to have a few special or difficult plants, grow them close to the house. The sight of them will remind you to look after them each time you walk in your door and they will be close by for easy maintenance.

Picture: Lorna Rose

EASY CARE GARDENING

Geraniums and daisies are two of the easiest to grow, longest flowering plants you can choose. Both come in a huge range of pretty colours and sizes. The garden in the picture above is situated in a cool climate where the winters are just frosty and the summers mild.

Cascading colour

The clean, sharp lines of this building, tall and stark against the sky, are stunningly contrasted with this huge, wonderful mound of cascading Pelargoniums, ivy geraniums and daisies which softly engulf the house. Pale pinks and hazy whites lead the eye through the picture. A concentrated splash of bright pink and vermilion frames the gate, and the rounded big pink rose bush, exuberant in health, adds a firm note of deep green.

TIPS FOR SUCCESS

Fuss free gardening

Easy care plants have long flowering habits, are pest and disease resistant and are attractive out of season with their foliage, fruit and seed.

Choose the right plants for the job. Grow swamp-loving plants in damp spots and desert plants in dry ones, rockery plants on rocks and seaside plants by the sea. It's easy!

Have simple planting schemes with only a few varieties of plants.

Don't expect your garden to be as spotless as your kitchen. Take pleasure in fallen leaves and petals and use them for mulch or compost later on.

Make room for each plant so that it can grow to its natural shape and size without pruning.

Keep lawn space to a minimum. Think of all that mowing (and weeding, feeding, fertilising and aerating). Trees and shrubs are a lot less work.

If you are going to have lawn, make it wide enough for the lawn mower. Make your lawn a simple shape without angular corners that are difficult to cut. And edge it with paving, concrete or timber so that trimming it is easy.

Ensure that your lawn does not get overly worn by making it large enough to walk across in several places.

Mass Planting

Many of us are used to looking at plants individually and mainly for their flowers. This is reflected in the impulsive way in which we buy them or are given them – when they are in bloom. We buy one lovely specimen and then try to find a place for it. After flowering the novelty wears off, or the plant is lost in the combined chaos of too much variety. This is the most common way in which our domestic gardens develop. Sometimes, in the hands of someone who knows what they want and why, it is a success but more often than not it is a failure.

A new approach to design

The opposite of planting one of each species is to plant many of the one species. This approach to gardening is called mass planting. It may seem an impersonal idea but it is a desirable way to approach all planting whether large or small in scale, or formal or informal in style. Mass planting is a useful con-

cept for people who know little about plants and gardening. By choosing fewer varieties that do well in your area and using masses of them, you'll minimise the risk of plant failure and unwise combinations. Your garden will be easier to maintain, too. But mass planting is not just for beginners. Planting lots of one type of plant does not reflect a lack of knowledge or imagination; it takes a different sort of knowledge and imagination. It takes an appreciation of the qualities of a plant and an understanding of how these features may best be used.

Plants as architecture

Things look different when plants are massed. They no longer get lost in the garden. Every individual feature, such as plant shape, flower colour and leaf texture, is intensified. The plants become strong and dramatic, they become architectural.

In this chapter we discuss why and how we should use mass planting.

Blue on blue

Only two types of plants – lavender and *Osteospermum ecklonis* – but a mass of each
makes this harmonious combination. When planting different flowers it's best to plant
each species together to form a broad patch of that colour. This usually looks better than many
spots of different colours. However, with only two plants in complementary colours, a thorough mix of
the two, rather than separate bands of colour as shown here, would give a lovely, hazy effect. Notice how
the canopy of the trees makes a lime-gold ceiling over the whole scene, contrasting with the
flowers and reflecting the pale green of the summer lawn.

TAKING THE CONCEPT FURTHER

Without realising it, we all use mass planting in parts of our gardens in the form of hedges, rows of trees, lawns, drifts of bulbs and groups of shrubs. We can take this concept further by changing the way we combine shrubs in garden beds to create a strong formal or natural design.

Imagine farmland fields spread out like a patchwork quilt; orange groves planted in a grid or terraced hillsides of olives and vines. These are mass plantings on a large scale. The beauty of these scenes lies in the simple, formal repetition of one or a few elements of, for instance, trees, terraces and flowers.

Mimicking nature

In the wilderness it is rare to see one of each plant. Usually, many of the one species is found interspersed with masses of something else and the occasional individual plant.

Imagine the natural landscapes that you have seen: undulating sand dunes or sweeping prairies colonised with a few grasses, meadows blooming with one or two species of wildflowers, forests dominated by a handful of tree species. None of these landscapes is formal, yet they all contain many of the one plant. Massing, therefore, is a very natural style.

Creating drama

In a suburban garden we can have the drama and visual impact of those larger scenes by combining plants in masses. With repetition and a sweeping layout, we can mimic the larger landscape.

In your garden let groups of plants represent the hills and valleys of your imaginary wilderness scene. Let the pretty foliage flow like streams or meandering lines. Your "meadow" may be in a courtyard with a single tree, a seat and a carpet of flowers and ornamental grasses. Your "stream" may be a sinuous line of thickly planted water Iris, as pictured at right. Your "hillside" may be mounds of lavender with paving or a ground cover as its foreground.

Bold and beautiful ▶

The red and yellow flowers in this scene contrast with the clear blue sky and green landscape behind. The large amount of yellow in the form of Arctotis flowers is needed to balance the more intense and sparsely spaced red flowers of the coral tree (*Erythrina x sykesii*). The red compensates in depth of colour for what it lacks in volume.

◀ A single sweep of yellow

These Iris seem to march forever, their yellow faces awash in a current of upright leaves. In this low-lying, boggy part of the garden many different colours of water Iris or types of bog plants could have been used. Instead, a single variety has been massed to make a simple but strong splash of colour.

TIPS FOR SUCCESS

How to choose plants for mass planting

Some plants are more suited to mass planting than others. Remember, every feature a plant has will be multiplied a hundred or thousand fold if you are going to mass it.

Ensure that all parts of a plant's natural cycle are attractive or not unattractive. You want to be sure that your grouping is not going to involve acres of staking, dead heading, dividing or tip pruning on a frequent basis.

Dead flowers remaining on a plant for days or weeks look unappealing in large quantities. This feature is an advantage only in plants whose dying flowers, seed heads or fruit is an attractive feature.

Select plants which require infrequent maintenance, then the chores that are required can be done in blocks. There may be occasional spraying for pests or annual or twice annual pruning. It is easier to tackle a whole area at once than attend to the needs of several individual species.

Keep in mind the number of formal hedges you have and how fast the shrubs that make them up grow. You don't want to be forever pruning.

Remember that tall hedges need to be maintained with ladders.

Select hardy varieties. Any failure will be magnified by the number of plants you use. If plants in a large area look sick or die, it can leave an unsightly space which will be expensive to replant.

▲ Blue ribbon

A hedge of blue Agapanthus provides a planted addition to the top of a retaining wall. The globes of blue flowers on upright stems and the glossy, strappy leaves form textured ribbons of green and blue. They help screen the property from below while allowing more distant views out from within the garden. Used in this way, the planting is like a balcony railing or balustrade.

▲ Variation on a theme

A collection of various colourful daisies spills down this slope, punctuated in hazy patches by clumps of perennial wallflowers and Iris. A variation on the mass planting theme, instead of one type of plant it's basically one family – daisies – all of similar texture and height, but varying flower colour.

MORE EFFECTS OF MASSING PLANTS

There is no denying the drama and impact of planting in masses. The pictures in this chapter show some of the sensational effects of large quantities of a colour or leaf texture in gardens.

Areas of planting define spaces, just as walls do. This is more boldly achieved with massed groups of flowers, shrubs or trees. See how two lines of orange Kniphofia on page 24 define the road so sharply, how the yellow carpet of Arctotis daisies on page 25 creates strength and drama. Remember all the clipped hedges of yew and box you have seen, tall walls of conifers, areas of lawn or patterns of parterre, and how well they outline a space.

The key to mass planting is simplicity. Massing creates a striking picture and reduces the distractions of having many different things to see. Without distractions you can notice other effects of the plants; their uniformity allows you to see the shape of the ground beneath low plantings while they follow every contour. This is not apparent in a planting with many different specimens of varied heights. Uniform planting magnifies the beauty of an individual plant, turning it into a breathtaking mass of colour.

Do not be frightened by the thought of monotony. Mass plantings are rarely monotonous. Be bold and try it; see how dramatically it will change your garden and simplify maintenance. You would have to try very hard to make a mass planting unsuccessful!

▲ Not all combinations work

When choosing plants to mass together, it is best to select species that require the same conditions that you are offering. Here Asplenium ferns in the foreground and tree ferns behind, both from shady, rainy, forested areas, look out of place with the grass trees, Croweas and Grevilleas of drier, sunnier, harsher environments. The ferns are suffering from too much sun, not enough water, and soil that lacks the humus of forest floors. But if you give the ferns more shade, more water and more humidity, you may kill the drier climate plants.

Paperbark maple

The finest gold leaf could not peel in more sculpted curls than the exquisite bark of the paperbark maple (*Acer griseum*). Beneath the copper coloured peels, the satin surface of new bark is revealed. Warm and rich, this beautiful trunk gleams in the spring sunshine of a cool climate garden.

Tree Trunks

DESIGNS AT EYE LEVEL

Due to their size, trees dominate a garden. They are taller than most other elements and often broader. In groups or by themselves, they can define the shape and structure of your garden.

Just as the texture and colour of walls influence the style and atmosphere inside your home, so outside do the shape, colour and texture of trees and their trunks direct the mood of the garden.

Tree trunks are as varied and interesting as the trees themselves. They are wonderful to look at and often surprising to touch.

Endless variety

When you start noticing tree trunks you find an endless variety of them – rough, smooth, peeling or flaky in texture, straight, twisted or gnarled in shape. They may be thick or thin, pale or dark, single standing or in clusters.

By planting trees with appealing trunks, you can create a particular feeling throughout the garden or in just one part of it.

Experience light and enchantment as you pass amongst a grove of pale, slender trunked trees. Feel the mystery and solemnity invoked by a dusky glade of pine or turpentine (Syncarpia). Appreciate them in all lights and weathers – early on a dewy morning, against a grey sky, mellow in the afternoon sun or glistening after rain.

Eye level importance

Of course, choose trees for their size, shape and flowers but don't neglect the eye level importance and attraction of the trunks. Tree trunks can add a special richness of colour and texture to your garden. To start your imagination flowing, this chapter explores wonderful ways with tree trunks, including the use of epiphytes, plants that grow on trees.

TREES WITH BEAUTIFUL BARK

FOR COOLER CLIMATES:

Acer davidii, A. pensylvanicum (snakebark maple)

Arbutus x andrachnoides

Pinus roxburghii (chir pine)

Populus tremuloides (quaking aspen)

Prunus maackii (Amur chokecherry)

Prunus serrulata (Japanese cherry)

Stewartia pseudocamellia (Japanese Stewartia)

Ulmus parvifolia (Chinese elm)

FOR WARMER CLIMATES:

Acacia spectabilis (Mudgee wattle)

Angophora costata (smooth barked apple)

Banksia serrata (saw Banksia)

Caesalpinia pulcherrima (leopard tree)

Chorisia insignis

Eucalyptus niphophila

Lagerstroemia indica (crepe myrtle)

Melaleuca quinquenervia (paperbark tree)

Sabal palmetto

ATTRACTION OF EPIPHYTES

Epiphytes are plants which grow on trees. They are not parasites, they merely attach themselves to their hosts and cause no harm. Among the types of plants available are epiphytic orchids, bromeliads and ferns.

Use them to bring eye level interest to unremarkable tree trunks and to add an extra layer of variety to your garden.

Many epiphytes come from rainy, misty, humid forests. In gardens they may need regular misting and an occasional feeding with very diluted liquid organic fertiliser. Other ephiphytes, including many Tillandsias and some orchids, are from seasonally dry tropical and subtropical forests and you should not feed or water them during their dry season.

Climbers an option

Another way to decorate a tree trunk is to use a very lightweight climber. These plants have small leaves and never grow rampant. They won't completely cover the trunk nor shoot up into a tree's canopy as do the other climbers. A good example is the maidenhair vine pictured at right, but there are also climbing ferns which may suit your garden.

Trees for epiphytes

Epiphytes won't harm a tree but the host's needs must still be taken into account. If you cover a tree from a dry climate with rainforest epiphytes, the introduced plants' needs for constant water will conflict with the tree's expectations of dryness.

Generally speaking, rainforest trees are happy to play host to epiphytes. In fact, most trees will support epiphytes, the major exception being those that shed their bark.

Catching on

Epiphytes may be attached to trees directly or on mounting boards. Do not loop any material such as wire around trunks or branches because over time this will strangle the tree to death. Few of us remember to remove or enlarge the wire later on so it's best not to try it. Rather, attach your plant using glue, plastic budding tape or twine made from a decomposable, natural fibre.

For cooler climates ▶

The temperate rainforests of the world are home to many epiphytes and climbers, the maidenhair vine among them. It is a lightweight, deciduous vine from New Zealand which looks lovely against wet, lichen-covered trunks in moist gardens. It will tolerate lows of at least -5˚C (23˚F).

Tree full of bird's nests

Sheltered beneath an evergreen tree's canopy are these lush bird's nest ferns (*Asplenium nidus*). From tropical to near frost-free areas, they can be attached to shaded or partially shaded branches. Their cupped leaves must be upright in order to collect rain and falling leaves (which rot to feed the plant). Young plants will grow from spores dropped or washed into the crevices of rough barked trees.

Temple of the trees

You can almost smell the resinous scent of this little pine forest. Outside, the wind may howl and the rain may fall but inside this copse, amongst the dark trunks, there is the quiet calm of a church. A dusty light filters through the copse, invoking a feeling of great age. Groups of any closely spaced trees can create this atmosphere and, where space permits, a copse is an unusual and powerful addition to the garden.

Lorna Rose

AVENUES AND COPSES

The collective effect of tree trunks and branches, lined up in an avenue or arranged in copses, can be breathtaking. If you have one tree with a beautiful trunk, imagine how much more beautiful it would be repeated in a formal or informal grouping.

An avenue is best attempted in a larger garden, along a long driveway, for example, but a copse can be successful in a smaller space, especially if the trees chosen are relatively slim and compact.

"Merry Garth", garden of K & E Raines

Startling copse ▲

Five closely planted silver birches (**Betula pendula**) make a startling copse against this dark background of evergreen foliage. In copses, an odd number of trunks looks best.

Rainforest relics ▶

These aged Sassafras trunks still carry the moss and lichen picked up when this garden was a rainforest. The trees are enhanced by the extra layer of interest these plants provide.

◀ **Posy of Pleasure**

This petite assortment of creamy yellow Violas, Felicia daisies and bright candy pink Petunias would make a happy picture anywhere – in a pot, windowbox, urn or planter. Here, their upturned faces in soft, bright colours fill a tiny spot in a patio bed.

Welcome home! ▶

For weeks in spring and summer this little bed gives a warm welcome with a pretty and fragrant colour combination. A healthy specimen of the rose 'Iceberg' is the big name in this duo, its sweet, white flowers contrasting with the underplanting of catmint.

Picture: Leigh Clapp Designer: Peter Fudge

Formal Gardens

Whereas a natural style of garden mimics nature, in a formal garden nature is tamed. Only a few different types of plants are grown in lines, blocks or patterns and they are kept to uniform sizes and shapes by pruning or shearing.

Owners of formal gardens do not need a wide knowledge of plants because they will only use a few types. Nor do they need to be enthusiastic gardeners; apart from clipping, formal gardens can be relatively easy to maintain. But the results, as we demonstrate in this chapter, can be diverse and impressive.

The power of two

This pretty, two-tiered border around a sundial uses just two plants – lavender and Erigeron. This garden could be fitted into a small courtyard and when the row of cypress in the background matures, the paved area will become a private, sheltered and very usable space. Lavender and Erigeron are easy to grow in temperate climates and need little attention other than an annual shearing.

TIPS FOR SUCCESS

Designing a formal garden

A formal garden relies on a geometric layout. Lines and shapes should be clean, bold and strong so that even if they are softened by overgrown foliage, they will remain apparent.

As formal gardens are designed in patterns, a pattern should first be drawn in plan on graph paper. Draw your ideas to scale and include the outline of your house and any other structures that you have.

Relate the layout of your formal garden to something important, like the features of your house: line up the main path with the front door; centre ornaments or path junctions under windows; or mimic the line of a facade with a hedge or path.

Be bold and simple with the construction and planting. For instance, a straight path with a hedge either side does not need a raised stone or brick edge for emphasis. Rather, spend your time making sure that a straight line is straight, a circle is round and a square is square. This is the kind of detail that is important.

Remember the height and width to which each plant will grow and do not over plant. You'll save hours of pruning; you'll also save money on the unnecessary purchase of many plants where fewer would do.

Avoid too many different features which separately draw the eye – statues, birdbaths, clipped or topiarised shrubs, urns, columns, plinths, arbours. Each has its uses but restraint is necessary. Otherwise, after a lot of expense, your garden will look like a shop.

Do not plant three layers of plants where there is really only room for one. Have one broad garden bed instead of two narrow ones. Formality does not require pairs.

Make beds wide enough to allow for growth. Remember, the plants will not remain the size they were when you bought them.

Blend of styles ▶

Here is an example of a formal garden informally planted. Although the layout is strictly geometric and each bed is enclosed with a clipped box hedge, the planting is as wild as that of a country cottage. A sea of colourful flowers spills from every bed onto the paths; they even drown out the young edges of box. However, with maturity this edging will enclose each bed like a full basket of flowers, creating a scene of soft formality.

Rodney Hyett

40

◀ **Tranquil simplicity**

Simplicity of the layout and planting is the key to this tranquil, easy to maintain garden which contains only three types of plants. There is generosity in the comfortable, wide box hedging, pleasure in the silver birch trees planted in each square, and a fullness in the planting of Agapanthus which rises above the hedges.

SHADES OF SHADE

The amount of light determines what you can grow in a particular spot. For instance, light levels beneath a densely foliaged evergreen tree with branches that sweep almost to the ground may be so low that nothing will grow, whereas the dappled shade under a high-branching, open foliaged tree may be bright enough for a huge variety of plants. In between there are countless degrees of shade. The more complete the shade, the fewer the plants you will be able to grow.

Part-shade occurs where the sun shines directly for a few minutes or hours and then moves away. Depending on how much sun there is and the time of year, these spots will be more or less suited to shade lovers.

To complicate matters, there is seasonal variation. Some gardens are blessed with sun in winter and shade in summer while others are cursed with winter shade and summer sun.

Degrees of shade affect the kind of plants that will thrive. Part sunlight or dappled light is necessary for many of the woodland flowers and shrubs like forget-me-nots and azaleas. Delicate, leafy plants which burn in direct light prefer the soft and even quality of indirect light. Plant species accustomed to the dark recesses of a tropical or cool climate rainforest floor will thrive in deep shade.

Dappled shade ▶

This spot, in bright but full shade, is an ideal home for the big, pleated leaves of a blue-leafed Hosta. Although these plants do produce pendulous, bell-like flowers on erect stems, they are grown more for their leaves which may be plain or variegated. In this kind of shade, lush clumps of ferns and many purple-leafed and variegated plants could be planted for greater richness in colour and leaf shape.

Part-shade ▲

Under a spreading deciduous tree, this bed is sunny in winter and shady during the middle hours of the day in the warmer months. If you have a spot like this, take your lead from this gardener with a mass of the spreading ground cover *Ajuga reptans* and part-shade tolerant flowers such as Aquilegia and honesty. Along the outer edges of the canopy, sun lovers such as lilies happily accept a few hours noonday shade in summer.

Garden at Lilianfels Resort

Designer: Malcolm Fletcher

Right at home ▲

Statuary can invoke romance in a garden when the subject is endearing and suits its environment. Here a pair of attractive stone deer look right at home in the thickly planted surroundings. The grain of truth in this setting adds credibility to the romantic fantasy.

Romantic roses ▶

Roses are the most romantic of all flowers, especially the sprawling, old-fashioned shrubs and climbers. Their habit of clambering and covering gives gardens a soft, informal look and when grown over or near a structure, the roses soften its outline. In turn the structure allows a beautiful presentation of the roses.

Romance of the classics ▲

Unlike the stone deer camouflaged in the woods, classical figures are meant to stand out, to be visible points of interest. They are often placed at the ends of paths or long views or as the centrepiece of a particular garden bed. Here the nymph, appealing in herself, is made more charming by the appropriate setting – a pool in a clearing in the forest. She brings a human element to the scene and through her presence we can imagine ourselves discovering and using such a lovely spot.

◄ Outside looking in

No glass is needed to feel the separation between the two garden worlds on either side of this window. At this time of day, the bright, sunlit courtyard on the "other side" beckons. The glimpse through the window, with its frames intact, creates curiosity and a desire to enter the room.

Where to? ►

A closed door. Perennials slow the way, growing over the path and narrowing it. A strip of sky and distant hills is glimpsed above the door. There is a strong sense of mystery and a desire to open the door. Where does it lead?

WALLS MEAN MICROCLIMATES

Microclimates mean opportunities

The walls in these pictures bring to mind the subject of microclimates. A microclimate is created when an object like a wall, an overhang, a boulder or a tree, changes the climate in its immediate vicinity. Of course, it will not change the elements – sun, wind and rain – but it may alter their effects, perhaps providing shade or shelter, creating a calmer, warmer, cooler, wetter or drier atmosphere. It all depends on which way the object faces in relation to the sun and prevailing winds.

Ways to use microclimates:

- Plants growing against a sunny wall receive radiated warmth long after the sun has set, allowing warmer climate plants to be grown in cooler climates.

- In a hot climate, radiated heat may be too intense, burning plants that would usually grow in that climate. If so, try plants from the world's deserts there.

- Obviously, every wall has two sides. While one side may be sunny most of the day, the other will be shady. The shady side will be cooler and more moist and may be ideal for ferns and woodland or understorey plants.

- Walls, boulders, trees and structures can create rain shadows in their lees, making it possible to grow drier climate plants.

- Walls may protect against wind, providing shelter and support for twining, scrambling and soft-stemmed plants unable to support themselves, or those which may be battered in more exposed conditions.

▲ Ruin reclaimed

Flowers scramble, climbers creep and perennials thicken, reclaiming the old building for nature. While you probably don't have such a structure, you may have a group of boulders or a big rock shelf that could perform a similar function. Such features would shelter and protect plants and also have a strong sculptural presence.

White is right

The snow white of azaleas, opaque white of candytuft and opal white of windflowers show the subtle variations in shade in a white planting. There is yellow here too, in the flower centres and a little discord in the form of a bluebell or two. White is the most popular choice for single colour gardens; it is tranquil, subdued, goes with almost any house colour, and white flowers look lovely at night. It is hard to go wrong with white.

Colour Schemes

Like paint in the home, colour is one of the most flexible and easily manipulated elements in the garden. But its very attraction contains a pitfall – it forms the basis of the impulse buy.

Few of us can resist the temptation of a plant with a pretty flower and we are encouraged in this because many plants are only sold in their flowering season. We take the pretty plant home and then try to find a spot for it. This is how we end up with randomly coloured gardens with no overall effect or, worse, nightmares of clashing colours jumbled together in a gaudy mix.

You can avoid both and create a better looking garden in the process if you settle on a colour scheme, then choose plants to suit it.

Stand back and contemplate

When choosing a new colour for your garden, stand back and take in the big view of your garden. Perhaps an extra colour would make it more interesting or would soften a combination that is too bright. The new colour might link together two colours which clash. Or maybe you need to reduce the number of colours you have together or grow each of them in larger patches.

Of course, you will need to know when the new plant flowers and whether or not it can live in the spot you have in mind. If you then decide to go ahead with your idea after these considerations, it will be an informed experiment with a greater chance of success.

SINGLE COLOUR GARDENS

Flower gardens or beds in a single colour are currently popular and, although white is a fashionable choice, any colour can be successful. You might choose a colour that matches your house, or pick your favourite colour.

Having settled on the colour, you might try to achieve just the one hue or use a variety of plants in different shades of that colour. The former will be quite hard unless you choose white or use a lot of the same plant.

If you decide to plant a single colour garden, odd splashes of a contrasting or complementary colour can look very effective; drifts of white flowers or grey leaves, for instance, can give a single colour planting a real lift by separating different plants of the same colour.

PLAYING WITH COLOUR

Colour expresses our emotions and it colours our moods. Some of the words we use to describe colour reflect this – loud, bright, happy, cheerful, mellow, tender, cool, blue, tranquil or sober. So with colour we have a powerful way to design our gardens, intensifying visual beauty with mood and feeling.

In a garden we can use colour to create passion and drama, ceremony or quietude, to weave a soft and pretty picture or a dazzling scene. The predominance of a certain colour or colour effect at a particular time of the year can become a tradition which reflects and enhances the season to which it belongs. For instance, bright, fresh pastels embellish spring; hotter, more vibrant shades or cool, nautical blues and whites strengthen a summer; and burgundy, scarlet, orange and gold adorn an autumn.

Part of the attraction of colour is this potential for seasonal transience, according to how long the plant remains in leaf or flower.

Colour sense

Theories for combining colour abound – how and what to mix and why. Some people think that pink and yellow don't mix, others believe orange is too garish for the garden. But in the end the use of colour, being one of the most emotive and subjective elements of a garden, comes down to personal taste.

◀ **Bright and beautiful**

The brilliant, inky colours of these flowers draw the eye from afar with their fiery intensity. For some of us, they paint a mood of summer passion. Long flowering through spring and summer and hardy in hot dry climates, Kalanchoe also comes in the softer sunset colours of apricot, yellow, peach and pink. They are small succulent plants, perfect for windowboxes or sunny, dry spots.

◀ **Cool climate spring**

Clear primary colours mixed with white always look cheerful and fresh. Here, the clear deep yellow of Geum blends with the opaque, crisp white of Nigella in a sunny juxtaposition. The touch of pinky-red in the background adds warmth to the scene. These are the light, candy colours of spring and early summer in a cool climate.

Brent Wilson

▲ Clearly autumn

A stunning example of colour and association, these deciduous trees are everything an autumn should be. The vermilion, orange and golden yellow canopies glow in spectacular beauty against a grey sky. A good autumn foliage display requires mild, sunny days and crisp, clear nights. Only where night temperatures fall sharply to near freezing or below can you expect a display as brilliant as this one.

▲ Guaranteed success

In the mellow light of a spring morning a collection of russet and gold blooms (Genista) glows like a sunrise. Planting a group of different coloured forms of the same species guarantees a consistency in leaf and flower texture that allows the colour effect to star. And you can be fairly certain that they will all flower at once.

ELEMENTS THAT AFFECT COLOUR IN A GARDEN

Remember there are some natural elements that will affect the colour that you choose for your garden. These include the quality of light and your distance from a plant. Some of this has been covered in part in the chapters "Views and Vistas" and "Small Spaces", but for convenience they are summarised here:

■ The angle of the sun affects the way we see colour. Vertical light is harsher and brighter on the eye and makes it harder to see any subtlety. Pale colours, for instance, appear washed out and only bright colours will withstand the effect. Conversely, diffuse, horizontal light allows soft colours to be seen in all their subtlety. In this soft light, bold, bright colours, when seen in their completeness, may appear gaudy.

■ The angle of the sun changes with the hour, month and latitude, so the geographical location of your garden, the time of day and the season will all influence which colours look best in your garden and when.

■ The texture of a leaf or flower surface, whether matt and absorbent or shiny and reflective, will alter the effect of the colour. Compare velvet, silk and cotton with the same shade of green to see the difference.

■ The effect of distance is to blur colour into a soft haze of blues and purples, greys and browns. Colour can therefore be used to create a sense of distance or to bring things apparently closer. For instance, use bright, bold colours (like bright yellow or red) to foreshorten, or pale, deep colours (deep blues, purples, silver and brown) to lengthen.

◀ **Variation on a theme**

Blues, purples and pinks have pigments in common. Here they have been combined in a shady corner with splashes of white and silver – additions which lighten and brighten the scheme. Dwarf red maple (*Acer palmatum* 'Atropurpureum') is underplanted with two types of *Lamium maculatum* and blue forget-me-nots. In the background the red stems of *Acer palmatum* 'Senkaki' can be seen.

▲ **Tranquil colours**

Instead of many different colours, just two shades of grey and dusky pink are blended to create this pastel coloured planting with a quiet mood. The pink flowers are African daisies (Arctotis); the taller, lighter grey foliage is possibly Artemis although any grey-leafed perennial would create the same effect.

THE MEANING OF COLOUR

Bright colours will generally excite, whereas deep or pastel colours will calm and subdue. Whether we like or dislike such effects depends on our mood or sensitivity and on our cultural associations.

In some cultures white represents marriage, in others it stands for mourning. Red can signify danger, glory, power, passion, lust or love. One can generalise and say that white is sobering or calming and red exciting to our emotions. A combination of red and yellow may be bright, bold and happy to one person and jarring and gaudy to another, but it is always stimulating. Pale pink and white may seem tranquil and pretty, or sickly and insipid, but it is always subdued.

Often the most successful and pleasurable colour combinations are the least contrived. These are the ones arrived at by instinct, spontaneity and a touch of flair.

◄ Mostly blue

A small patch of pink lupins acts as a warm highlight in a blue sea of forget-me-nots and borage. The pink of the lupins complements the blue borage flowers and the blue-green of the background foliage merges the blues together. In soft, low-angled light like this, pastel colours can be seen at their best.

Paths & Steps

Immortalised in sayings and songs, paths are the vital threads which hold garden designs together. Paths show us through a garden. They provide the means by which you determine what is seen, what is not seen and how it is seen.

Paths are designed to guide or misguide you, depending on their style and location. For instance, you may travel directly and purposefully to a destination on a straight, broad path, or your way may be ambling, narrowed by overspilling plants, slowed by irregularities of surface and beset with glimpses and views at every bend. Your experience is as much what you pass through as what you find at the end.

Practical paths

Paths usually have a practical purpose, leading you along well-used, necessary routes through the garden, such as from the front gate to the front door, or from the laundry to the clothesline. These paths should be as direct and broad as possible, not necessarily straight but not unnecessarily curved.

Making a feature of the path, instead of making it as small as possible, creates opportunities to include the path properly in your garden picture. It may need to take the shortest route between destinations but its width still can be generous enough to allow for both comfortable walking and the softening, pretty effect of overhanging foliage and flowers.

Taking shape

You can accentuate a path with hedges, colourful border plants or features such as arches or tubs of shrubs or flowers. Such features help to shape the garden path, determining the picture of your garden and how it is seen.

In this chapter we explore paths; where to position them, what shape they should take and which surfaces to use. And along the way, wherever there are changes in levels, we find opportunities to create interest with steps.

Step through the flowers

Rather than steps, this gardener used stepping stones to gradually climb the slope. Each stone is slightly higher than the one below, creating a lovely little path that you could imagine as a natural dry watercourse. A selection of slow, mat-forming alpines invades the spaces between the stones but as the feet of every passing walker wears them down, they will never grow across the steps. The mauve flowers on the left side are thrift (*Armeria maritima*).

Accentuate the positive ▶

A crimson ribbon of pinks (Dianthus) makes a seasonal display, accentuating the serpentine curve of this broad pathway. Where the curving outline is a feature, it is a nice idea to emphasise a path with a little clipped hedge, neat border planting or a long band of colourful flowers. The use of plants which spill over the edge would only obscure the strong curve. Colourful annuals only last for one season, so plant something behind them, such as the prostrate juniper (*Juniperus conferta*) shown here.

An even surface that is easy on the feet is the best choice for frequently used paths. Concrete, bricks, stone or pavers are possibilities and can be impressed with or laid in stylish and appealing patterns. Laid well on solid foundations, these surfaces will last a lifetime. If laying unit pavers, remember that the edge of the path locks the pavers in place, preventing them from sliding apart. It is very important that the edge be cemented into place.

PREFERRED ROUTES

The route a path should take is usually the most direct. If a track has already been worn to a destination, then that is the best route for a proper path. If, instead of following this desired approach, you make the path meander, you may irritate the users and encourage them to take short cuts.

Conversely, if an existing path takes an awkward route and a short cut is being worn, you could formalise the short cut into a proper path and dig up the existing route, giving it over to garden space.

Not all paths have a vital, everyday purpose. Some are for garden strolls, pleasure, and access to all parts of the garden for maintenance. These paths can be straight, wide and formal if you wish or they can be winding, still solidly paved or more casually built of gravel, rammed earth, stepping stones or bark chips.

Designed to charm

Paths for strolling along are meant to charm you with their quirks, such as dense shrubberies which enclose or partly conceal a view, fallen petals along the way, irregularities of natural stone in the surface and twists and turns in the route. There is no hurry to reach a destination so there can be hidden surprises – such as a statue or special plant – at the places where you are made to slow down. This may be where the path narrows or curves or where there is an uneven surface. Without creating an obstacle course, such surprises can be used creatively to control your speed of travel, direct your eyes to a particular scene and determine the atmosphere of that part of the garden.

◀ **Follow the red
brick road**

This path, with its
clearly defined edge
and attractive surface
of patterned
brickwork, firmly
leads you onward.
Although you cannot
see the destination
around the gentle
curve, confidence that
you will not be led
astray is inspired by
the clean lines, ample
width and neatly
maintained edge.
Direct in its route, this
path makes for an easy
trip to the front door,
thanks to its width,
regular surface and the
absence of
overhanging plants.

LAWN
MEETS PATH

*Where your lawn meets a
path, it is important that
there is no hard, raised edge
to impede mowing and
edging of the lawn. The path
should be flush with, or very
slightly below, the level of the
lawn. If the path must be
raised above the lawn, have
a mower strip between the
grass and raised edge.*

STEPPING OUT

Grand or charming, imposing or quaint, steps mark a transition, a managed progression through the garden. They may run between your entrance and the home, between one part of the garden or terrace and another, or ease your way across sloping ground. Teamed with views, arbours, ornaments or special plants, steps are gateways for change.

Steps, especially those frequently used, should be of comfortable, safe and attractive proportions. Poorly designed, uncomfortable steps can inhibit your use of a certain part of the garden.

Rainforest garden steps ▶

Fashioned from mossy tree fern trunks and the occasional boulder, these steps have become a garden in themselves. Overtaken by slow-growing alpine ground covers, the effect is cool, lush and serene. It leads the eye gently with colour and texture to the velvety sward of lawn above.

STEPS TO SUCCESS

Points to remember when building steps

The risers should be of the same height, except in very informal, boulder type steps which resemble stepping stones.

The maximum desirable number of steps in an unbroken flight is 14. If level changes are only slight, install two steps rather than one as one riser can be easily tripped over.

A reliable guide for step proportions is that twice the riser height plus the depth of tread should equal 68cms (27in), ie, 2r + t = 68cms (27in).

In addition to the above calculation, the minimum desirable riser height is 10cms (4in), the maximum for comfort is 17.5cms (7in), and the minimum tread depth is 30cms (12in) – "foot sized", so you don't have to walk crablike up or down, which is dangerous as well as uncomfortable.

In certain situations, the rules can and often are broken to good effect, but not without practical consideration first and not just for the sake of it.

Formal accent ▲

This flight of steps gains extra grandeur with a pair of urns on plinths positioned either side. For this to work, the steps should be rather formal in construction (as here) and relatively wide. Urns or statues can be placed at the top or bottom of steps. Allow them to be seen by not letting plants spread to obscure them too much. Here, encroaching flowers have narrowed the approach which should be as wide as the steps.

7 5

◄ Column of colour

A large-flowered Clematis hybrid offers an impressive welcome during its spring season and can be easily restricted to its supporting pillar. These plants need a cool to cold climate and a site where their roots can be kept cool, moist and shaded while the upper parts of the plant are exposed to full sun.

Flowering intrusion ▶

This home owner has no fear of flowers – they clamber over the steps and grow right up to the house between the cracks of a sandstone paved verandah. If this was the main entrance to the house this overgrowth would be impractical, but on these little used steps it is tolerated for the pretty, loose effect it creates. The grey-leafed ground cover is snow-in-summer (*Cerastium tomentosum*), the pink and white daisy at right is fleabane (*Erigeron karvinskianus*).

Freestanding feature wall ▶

A freestanding wall can be a strong design element. Here, a curved wall about halfway down the garden foreshortens the view from the house and focuses attention on the statue of Hebe. On the other, sunny side of the wall, a rose garden thrives in the shelter and reflected warmth. A billowing mass of 'Seaform' is the only clue to the rose garden's presence.

Retaining wall ▲

A striking and original feature has been made of this retaining wall using timber sleepers and local stone – materials that are available to many of us. But, in this combination, such common materials make a wall of individual character and considerable strength. The wall is the feature, without the distraction of plants or ornaments. It is the star of this part of the garden.

Appealing partnership ▶

A high stone wall creates shelter and complete privacy in the garden in a stylish way. Its old, weathered surface is a perfect place for ivy to grow. Unlike timber, the stone will last for decades beneath the ivy. The bare stone makes a good background for climbing plants and wall-mounted ornaments. If you grow a self-clinging vine on an attractive masonry wall, do not allow it to completely cover the wall. You will appreciate the wall more, and display the plant better, if the plant is restricted.

**White on green
on white** ▶

A picture of cottage
freshness in green
and white: a white
house with white
climbing rose and
glossy green foliage.
The foliage between
the two whites
enhances the
brightness of the
flowers, separates
the two shades of
white and picks up
the green trim
on the house.

Garden of Polly and Peter Park

Plant as art

Here the background is the main attraction, the plant
an embellishment. The tiles, a memento of a trip to the
Middle East, are the only feature on a white painted
garden wall. The stem of ivy, trained as a delicate
frame, claims them as part of the garden.

▲ A hot combination

There is no sense in trying to cool the look of these terracotta tiles. It is better to underscore the summery mood with a planting of fiery colours. This gardener chose orange geraniums and bright yellow Violas. The juxtaposition of the Violas deepens the intensity of the geraniums and lifts the overall effect. The terracotta pots match the deeper tones of the background so completely that they allow the flowers to star.

◄ Sunshine in the shade

The yellow flowers of Japanese rose (*Kerria japonica*) stand out in sunny contrast to the rich russet of the painted timber. A white or pastel coloured wall here would reflect more light onto the plants but the beauty of the contrast would be lost. In shade and/or against dark colours, bright greens look greener and yellows deeper.

Garden Pictures

CREATE PRETTY COMPOSITIONS

As lovely as they are, plants alone are not enough to make a really interesting and satisfying garden. Throughout history people have added all kinds of ornaments and structures to their gardens and these days we follow suit, searching for that certain something to complete a garden picture.

In this chapter we are not concerned with major installations that have a big impact on the garden but with simple, inexpensive ways to create little garden pictures. Each is a charming scene on its own, almost a garden design in miniature. And the more little scenes you create, the richer the detail of your garden will be.

Decorative details

Ornaments weather but they don't die. They can be as permanent a feature as you wish or can be readily moved, creating interest in a different part of your garden in a new way. They may reflect seasonal changes. For instance, sculptural elements may be more fully revealed in winter's sparsity than in summer's verdure.

Ornaments can beautify a part of the garden where plants struggle or act as optical illusions. Like the props on a stage set, they give extra credibility to the scenes you create in the garden. For example, you can believe that the door shown overleaf really is a door to another part of the garden.

Unusual appeal

Unusual, unique or homemade ornamentation is often more appealing than the mass-produced, as the picture on page 98 demonstrates. They can have curiosity value and an aura of mystery about them; and their novelty can make your garden appear more interesting and imaginative. Don't forget to decorate your walls. Apart from the traditional half baskets, wall fountains and plaques, you could consider using mirrors to imply a window or door, or a trompe l'oeil latticework to give a sense of distance.

A near miss

**Right beside a path, this little scene is so subtle it is easy to miss.
An old concrete laundry tub finds a new home and use in the garden
as a water feature. Raised above ground level, the sides of the tub are
hidden by a skirt of mondo grass and a rim of variegated ivy.
Duckweed floats on the water surface and the variegated grassy
plant is *Acorus gramineus*.**

Drawing a blank ▲

A false doorway and threshold framed in Japanese sacred bamboo (*Nandina domestica*) creates the convincing scenario of being able to walk further through the garden. This is a wonderful way to use ornamentation in the garden. The doorway is an attractive feature in itself, and it leaves the impression that there's more to this garden than meets the eye.

CHOOSING GARDEN ORNAMENTS

Whether unusual or commonplace, ornaments can bring a refreshing contrast to the garden. A change from one plant after another, ornaments can be used in imaginative and pretty ways.

Don't go overboard with ornaments – too many in a garden can appear busy and distracting. As a rule, one or two good, well-placed pieces look better than a garden full of lesser items.

Consider the size of an ornament when placing it – a small birdbath may look lost in the middle of the lawn but just right in a confined space; a statue, overwhelmed in a garden bed, may look perfect beside a small pool, and its reflection will double its size.

▲ **Pretty as a picture**

This pretty setting, comprising plants chosen for their harmonious colours and placed to create a conical mound, is designed as an island bed to be viewed at every angle. The tallest plant, the white flowered *Viburnum plicatum*, sits in the centre with progressively lower-growing species around it. The urn, in complementary grey, humanises the scene, making a hard contrast to the soft surroundings. Other plants shown include blue Iris, geraniums and Delphiniums.

An Imperfect Match

A sandstone rockery has been attempted here with mixed results. The rockery looks un-natural; there is little variation in the sizes of the stones and their placement looks disorderly.

The planting is also problematic. The grassy ground cover is alpine moss (**Scleranthus biflorus**), a native of boggy patches in mountain meadows, while the grass trees come from dry, sandstone heaths or open forests at low altitudes. The heavy watering necessary for the alpine moss will quickly upset the grass trees. The loose disposition of the rocks means that soil and water will rapidly drain away – fine for the grass trees but not for a plant from bogs.

The heat and humidity of this garden's climate, intensified by reflection from the stone, is nothing like the high altitude chill of the natural habitat of the moss.

Better alternatives

Instead of the alpine moss, tufty plants which like the well-drained conditions should be used with these grass trees. Some possibilities for inclusion are fountain grass (**Pennisetum setaceum**), flax (**Phormium tenax**) or dramatic succulents such as Agave or Yucca.

◀ **Spiky and soft on the rocks**

At first glance this rockery is impressive, its mix of shapes and textures immediately eye-catching. The spectacular grass trees (*Xanthorrhoea australis*) contrast with the soft richness of alpine moss (*Scleranthus biflorus*) and the stone in this composition. But beware, this combination of plants is fraught with problems.

Simple Structures

In gardens there are two types of structures – the useful and the decorative – but with some clever and pretty ideas you can combine these two qualities.

Take the garden shed: we use it to hide the messy necessities of gardening but often the shed is ugly, too. It need not be because you can transform even the plainest shed with plants.

If, in the first place, you erect a better-looking, more sympathetic building than the average shed, so much the better; it will fit more easily into the garden. No-one needs to know that if you open the door, rakes, bicycles and tins of paint will fall out. If necessary make it bigger because, if it is good enough to feature, it need not be squeezed into the smallest possible space or hidden in a distant corner.

Adding ambience

Not all structures are utilitarian – gazebos, arbours, pergolas and pavilions also have a place in the garden. These can be useful structures in that they provide shelter, or support for climbing plants. But whether built with a purpose or for show, a well-built structure always adds a special atmosphere to a garden.

When designing a structure for your garden try to match it with the style of your home. This is especially desirable if you want to build a structure against or close to the house. In a larger garden where you may want it positioned well away from the house, you can introduce exotic contrasts and create a special atmosphere by choosing a style that is different to your house, rather like the cupola from another culture in the picture at right.

Eccentric charm

If you're handy with a hammer and nails you can stamp your own personality on the garden when you build your structures. This homemade roofed gate, built out of reused timbers and tomato stakes, has a curious, Indian Raj look which adds an exotic touch to the garden. The cupola is too small to give shade or shelter from the weather – it is built for decoration. Not every garden structure has to have a practical purpose, but everything practical can be made to look attractive.

Beauty and a beast ▶

Common to many gardens, the aluminium shed can really only be hidden. Here, the eye is distracted from its shiny surface by a striking duo of red and yellow roses. Even when out of bloom, the foliage of climbing 'Bloomfield Courage' helps to conceal both the shed's large size and surface. Painting the shed would also tone down the parts that will always show, such as the door.

Lorna Rose

In country gardens, old ramshackle buildings sometimes remain and wherever possible they should be incorporated into the landscape design. There is beauty in weatherworn timbers and iron, especially when partly obscured by a garden. Buildings like these are not junk; they are a living link with the district's past. They can be important in family history, too. The door of this one chronicles young Mal's ascendancy to head of the shed!

QUICK CLIMBERS TO CONCEAL

FOR COOLER CLIMATES

- *Trumpet vine (**Campsis radicans**), a vigorous North American evergreen vine with bright orange flowers appearing in summer.*

- *Clematis, a moderately vigorous deciduous vine which comes in a huge choice of flower sizes and colours. Flowers late spring or early summer.*

- *Climbing Hydrangea (**Hydrangea petiolaris**) is a fairly vigorous deciduous vine that clings with adhesive pads.*

- *Honeysuckle, deciduous and evergreen vines with fragrant spring and summer flowers. Rampant where winters are not very cold.*

FOR FROST-FREE CLIMATES

- *Golden shower (**Pyrostegia venusta**), a vigorous evergreen with masses of brilliant orange flowers in winter. Needs a warm, sunny spot.*

- *Chilean jasmine (**Mandevilla laxa**), a vigorous evergreen with fragrant white flowers.*

- ***Hardenbergia violacea**, a moderately vigorous evergreen climber with small purple flowers in pendulous clusters in spring.*

- *Star jasmine (**Trachelo-spermum jasminoides**), a glossy leaved evergreen with fragrant white flowers which appear in late spring. Grows fairly vigorously.*

Herbal parterre

This nursery in New Zealand has been laid out in separate gardens, each with a biblical theme. The herbal parterre shown is planted in the shape of a Star of David with lavender cotton (*Santolina chamaecyparissus*) forming one of the interlocking triangles and dwarf box the other. Thyme, tansy and Chrysocoma fill the centres of the triangles. A herbal parterre like this could be reduced to suit a space of about 6x6m (20x20ft).

Garden of Gethsemane

Garden Patterns

You may well ask what patterns have to do with gardens but patterns can be found everywhere. The selection and organisation of patterns is the basis of all picture making, garden pictures included.

In a garden we see patterns in the vertical pickets or overlapping palings of a fence, in pavers laid out across a terrace, in the shapes of garden beds, the colours and groupings of plants within the garden bed and the arrangement of different textures in a setting. The patterns work together to create the picture we see.

Many possibilities

When we design a garden we choose from a multitude of possible effects. We choose patterns of shape, colour and texture and weave them together to form a whole garden or a small scene.

Sometimes we do this instinctively but understanding what it is that underlies our choices can enable us to plan the garden more successfully. In this chapter we show you some exciting ways to use patterns in garden design.

Designer: Imperial Gardens

◄ **Hills and valleys**

The velvety folds of alpine moss
(*Scleranthus biflorus*) rise and fall like
rolling hills in miniature. This is a curious
plant, strikingly different from most
others thanks to its rich colour and
texture and mounding habit. It is from
snowy, alpine areas and likes a cool
climate and peaty, moisture-retentive soil.
It does not do well in humid,
warm-temperate or subtropical areas.

▲ **Pattern in paving**

Four types of stone in contrasting sizes,
colours and shapes create an eye-catching
pattern in paving. The smooth, dark
surfaces of the squared-off stepping
stones stand out from the white,
finer-textured background, and also
contrast with the adjacent river stones
and boulders. Such a strongly defined
path leads the eye through the garden but
the feet will almost certainly follow.

Painting in stone ▲

River stones, coloured gravel, rocks and brick edging have been used to paint a beach beside a garden pond. Stones and gravel can also be used in geometric or abstract patterns instead of ground covers or conventional paving. The idea works in small spaces, too.

Ground cover with a difference ▶

Lawns are often difficult to grow under trees. The foliage canopy shades the grass and the trees' roots compete with the grass for water and nutrients. In some instances, the water and fertiliser applied to the grass can be too much for the trees' good health. This gardener has solved such problems by removing the grass and replacing it with gravel. The bright white stones found naturally on the property throw the grass, foliage and flowers into sharp relief and fill the garden with brightness.

Garden Note

Consider the use of gravel or rock to make patterns and shapes in the garden, especially where underlying rock is close to the surface. Whether it be the white of chalk or limestones, creamy sandstones, the pinks and greys of granite or the rusty red of ironstone, the exposure of the underlying rock can be very striking and attractive.

Small Spaces

BEAUTY OF A SMALL GARDEN

Beauty lies not only in large vistas and grand gestures, but in the smallest, most intimate things. Small gardens are potentially intimate places made rich and pleasurable by the tiny pictures you create. In small gardens you can become enthralled by the beauty of a single flower or a light fragrance wafting through. These details occur in larger gardens too, but you may not notice them; they may disappear in the general effect. In the pretty confines of a small garden, details which are lost in the grand scale can be enjoyed.

Small gardens are more intensively used than larger ones. If a scene is beautiful in a small garden, it can give you pleasure a hundred times a day. There is no room for wasted space in a small garden; every detail is noticed. Paths, edges, arbours, gates and seats will be well-used, so they should be designed to withstand wear and tear as well as for viewing from close quarters. Every glance should be filled with pretty views and vistas.

Small pleasures

The advantage of having a small garden is its manageability. With good planning, a small garden allows you the privilege of as much care and maintenance as you desire, without it overwhelming you.

It enables you to indulge yourself with fragile or fussy plants that would represent troublesome chores if planted in larger numbers. And, whereas in larger gardens your time may be spent on acres of weeding, watering and lawn mowing, in a small garden even fiddly maintenance is quickly completed.

The small garden suits gardeners who love variety and detail as well as those who never want to nurture a fragile plant, but just want a green space where they can sit in a deck chair and read or have coffee in the morning sun.

In this chapter you will find pictured some beautifully simple small gardens and ideas for planning them.

Plan gone wrong

Designed to be seen from above, this garden started out as a pattern described by the formally laid out paths. However, the planting of the shrubs, in groups which are neither symmetrical nor random, breaks up the formality and the circular layout of the design. For a more pleasing result you could either make the planting more mixed, more informal or underscore the formal structure by planting the beds in a regular, symmetrical fashion.

ENLARGING SMALL SPACES

Nothing makes a garden look smaller than seeing the full extent of its boundaries. Just as walls of a room recede when you put furniture in it, so the walls of the garden appear further away when you grow shrubs and trees, or place garden furniture in front of the fence. This does not mean that you have to conceal the entire fence line, only part of it.

Trees in a small garden

Although placing trees in front of a fence takes up space, it makes the garden appear bigger by creating an impression of depth. If their branches are high enough to sit beneath, you will have the best of both worlds – space and an effect of distance.

A sense of balance is needed between the qualities and size of a tree or shrub and the size of the garden. A group of large plants, for instance, can suit a large garden if there is generous space between them. Practical considerations should also be taken into account. The plant must suit the space in every respect. In a small garden, a tree or shrub that is too large is more than unattractive; it is a menace and may be costly and difficult to remove.

Illusions of scale

Small items make a small garden appear bigger. This means using many small-growing, small-leafed and flowered trees and shrubs. It means small patterns on paved surfaces, paving with bricks on their edges, tiling with small tiles or using gravels with a fine texture. By reducing the scale of your materials, you make the space appear bigger.

From side passage to view garden ▶

This lush garden was created from a narrow, little-used passage between the house and the boundary fence. Shaded for most of the day, it is a perfect home for ferns, orchids and other shade lovers. Although there is a stepping stone path, it is more for essential access than regular use. The planting is meant to be seen from here.

◀ Jurassic garden

In this small courtyard only a few fairly big plants have been used, but they work thanks to the generous distance between each plant. The space between them produces a feeling of depth, whereas crammed full it would close in on you. The ferns, tree ferns, palms and cycads are all relics of the age of dinosaurs and grouped together they create an impression of a strange Jurassic lagoon. The plants also all have strongly sculptural forms which look lovely silhouetted against the white walls of the house.

◀ Use what you have

Natural seepage from the rocky ledge behind made this a boggy part of the garden. Rather than drain all the excess water away, these gardeners capitalised on what they had by turning boggy ground into a pond. By accident of landform, or because of structures, you may also have a unique site such as this. If a pool is your solution, don't make it too small or shallow. If you only have room for a small water feature, use a bowl, birdbath or small fountain.

TIPS FOR SUCCESS

Planning a small garden

First, identify the inclusions you need (paths, clotheslines, access to other parts of the house, storage shed, etc.) and those you would like to have (place to sit one, two, four or six people, particular plants, particular ornaments, etc.).

❧

Now decide on the purpose of the garden. Is it for looking at or for being in? Will there be several viewpoints or just the one? Once in it, what will you do there?

❧

Be flexible in your demands. Perhaps exchange the clothes hoist for a foldaway line. Maybe you usually only need to seat four people, so you can use a small table rather than trying to squeeze in six (except on special occasions).

❧

Be creative; make everything that is pretty do something useful. For instance, retaining walls or steps that can comfortably double as seats.

❧

Be selective in your choice of plants. No garden can grow everything, so revel in the pleasure of deciding what you will plant.

Mould plants to shape ▶

Small-leafed plants can become moulded decorative elements if you clip them into shapes. Here, a once straggly Cotoneaster which was destined for removal was saved by the transformation into a living awning. Clipped hedges and topiaried potted plants are additional ways to use the shears for decorative effects. Although clipping can be time consuming, in a small garden the amount of work involved is minimal.

Elegance and easy care ▶

This tiny courtyard looks green and inviting thanks to the clusters of big pots. The largest tubs house weeping figs and Citrus trees which create the impression of height and an overhead canopy. Smaller pots containing clipped box plants represent a shrubbery. The result is a simple, elegant garden that is easy to maintain. In a cooler climate you could replace the figs and Citrus with, say, maples and dwarf peaches or standardised gooseberries.

▲ Room with a view

A picture of serenity, this garden is like a beautifully arranged room. It is spacious yet intimate, open but private. The long city view and the neighbour's trees and shrubs, noticeable at left, create a feeling of unlimited space. Note the dividing wall with creeping fig (*Ficus pumila*); it also helps create the illusion that the garden continues on behind the bench. The small table and chairs in the far right corner blend perfectly into the dark green background. They provide a quiet place to sit and enjoy the garden from a different viewpoint.

Vegetables & Herbs

Culinary herbs and vegetables can be twice as lovely growing in the garden as they are served at the dinner table. Herbs can be freely planted to blend in with other shrubs, flowers and ground covers because they do not look out of place with ornamental garden plants. Rosemary is as much a shrub as is an azalea; pennyroyal mint or creeping thyme as much ground covers as violets or Ajuga.

The same is true of vegetables. They are equally at home in the ornamental garden as in the vegetable plot, providing they have a sunny spot. After all, vegetables have leaves and flowers too and, if you only want to grow a small selection, popping them into flower beds is a lot easier than digging up a new vegie patch.

Neat is pretty

In this small vegetable patch against a sunny trellised fence, a sensible array of taller vegetables behind (corn, beans, tomatoes or peas) and smaller ones in front (lettuce, carrot, cabbage, cauliflower) is decorated with an annual planting of marigolds. The marigolds look pretty and are said to keep soil nematodes away. This is an example of companion planting and shows how mixing vegetables with annuals can make the vegetable garden naturally healthy as well as appealing to the eye.

Starting a vegetable patch

Vegetables (like most flowering annuals) generally need full sun, or at least more than 4 hours' direct sun per day.

Vegetables need cultivated, well-drained soil. Raised beds help to provide this.

Vegetables have high water and nutrient requirements so they need generous helpings of rotted organic matter.

The vegetable plot should be almost as tidy as your kitchen. Minimise pest and disease damage and promote quality in your harvest by keeping vegetable beds weed free, and removing all dead matter for compost long before it rots next to the vegetables.

Take early action to control pests and diseases before they really take hold.

Avoid gluts and famines by staggering the planting of the same vegetables at intervals. Be practical in your harvest expectations; few of us intend to be self-sufficient.

Save space in the vegetable garden for vegetables which are the most unusual or expensive in the shops, or which benefit more than others by being eaten fresh – lettuce and tomatoes, for instance, as opposed to onions or potatoes.

VEGETABLES AS DECORATION

A well-tended vegetable patch has a beauty of its own in its rich soil, raised beds of earth and neat rows of sturdy plants. We take pleasure in the sight of tomatoes, peas and beans on canes and lettuce and strawberries snug beneath netting cloches. We find wholesome charm in the farmyard tangle of corn, the vigour of rhubarb and spinach and satisfying rosettes of cabbage and cauliflower. And we see beauty in the lacy foliage of carrot and asparagus and the striking flowers of onion, garlic and leek.

Enjoy all parts of the vegetables, not just the edible parts, as the leaves, flowers, buds and stems can be attractive in themselves.

Making features out of necessities can also improve the vegetable patch. You could decorate the edges of the vegetable garden with ornamental edging tiles, painted steel or bamboo hoops. Alternatively, you could use herbs, annuals and pretty hedges as border plants. You could also give your vegetable garden an attractive setting with a background of screening and ornamental plants. But ensure that these do not cast shade on the vegetables themselves.

Planted in neat rows or groups and embellished with flowers, herbs and tiny fences, a vegetable patch can be decorative as well as practical.

Green and practical ▶

In this detail of a vegetable garden, old tyres are put to good use. They are a convenient way to grow vegetables that need hilling or blanching (potatoes in this case). As the plants grow, another tyre is placed on top and more soil added. Unattractive in themselves, the tyres are cleverly concealed behind the healthy growth of sweet corn.

Bouquet garnis ▲

A potpourri of scented leaves and flowers spill over each other and tumble onto the path in a ready-made bouquet. Lavender, herb Robert (*Geranium robertianum*) and lemon balm (*Melissa officinalis*) blend with other herbs, including pinks (Dianthus), spearmint (*Mentha spicata*), and more. It shows a wonderful mix of useful and pretty herbs in a narrow garden bed. A backdrop of climbing herbs or vegetables (nasturtiums or peas, for example) would add to this pretty assortment and screen the fence behind.

> ### *Garden Note*
>
> *Rather than thinking of herbs and vegetables as separate from ornamental plants, it is useful to think of herbs as perennials and vegetables as annuals. This affects the way we grow them– annuals need better soil and regular food and water – and helps us to find pretty ways to use them.*

COMBINING HERBS IN THE GARDEN

The perennial nature of many edible and decorative herbs means they can be included as a long-term part of a general planting scheme or in a garden of their own.

A herb garden may take a formal shape, as in an elegant parterre with hedges of box, rosemary or lavender enclosing an aromatic mix of favourite culinary and medicinal herbs. Alternatively, it may have an informal look with herbs spilling over paths in the pleasant disorder of a country cottage. Herbs take many forms; for instance, bay is a tree, rosemary a shrub and thyme a ground cover. This means you can create a herb garden, complete with canopy, shrub layer and ground covers.

Mix and match

You can mix herbs with other ornamental plants or match them in a separate herb garden. For instance, clip bay trees for formal features or use them unclipped as small trees. Rosemary can be grown formally as a hedge or used naturally as the dense, rounded shrub it is. Tubs of basil, marjoram and lemon grass can be placed at the kitchen door or either side of a gate. Grow parsley for fresh greenery amongst your annuals. Mix garlic, chives and lemon balm with Iris, roses and lavender. Plant chamomile for tea and fragrance in beds, as a lawn or between stepping stones. Tread on a scented thyme carpet as you pick rosemary for the kitchen and lavender for the house.

WHAT IS A HERB?

*W*e all know what vegetables are, but when we talk about herbs as separate from other garden plants it is useful to know what they are.

*Botanically speaking, herbs are plants with non-woody parts. This means that many perennial and annual flowers are rightly called herbs by scientists. But in the language of gardeners, herbs are plants with aromatic or flavoursome flowers, seeds, leaves or roots. They are grown for culinary or medicinal uses, or simply for the fragrances they release into the garden. Whether they are woody or not is irrelevant; cooks are quite happy to include as herbs the aromatic bay tree and the rosemary shrub. Even succulents, such as **Aloe vera**, are considered herbs by those who use its gelatinous sap.*

So much for categories! In this chapter we are talking the language of gardeners, not botanists.

Fragrant footfall ▶

In this delightful scene, the spaces between these informal steps have been planted with various creeping thymes. Steps can be purposefully designed with spaces for plants while the steps make islands upon which to tread between the herbs. Walking on the herbs that stray over the steps keeps them naturally in place and releases a burst of aroma.

◀ Sweetness and spice

A living tapestry of culinary and ornamental herbs growing between pavers and gravel. One can almost smell the sweetness and spice rising from the plants. This part of the garden consists almost entirely of herbs — rosemary, thyme, catmint, oregano, chives and lavender. Other than keeping plants to their allotted spaces and watering in winter, it needs little attention.

Striking a blue note

A classical sundial, dark and reflective after an overnight shower, stands as the centrepiece of a pretty
mix of herbs and flowers. Here, borage and Artemis jostle for space with perennial poppies in a
colourful and aromatic planting that also provides cut flowers and culinary and cosmetic herbs. The use
of a traditional ornament is an attractive and clever way of blending useful herbs amongst the general
planting of a garden bed. By association, it gives the herbs an ornamental reason to be there.

TIPS FOR SUCCESS

Growing herbs successfully

- *The main requirement for growing herbs is to give
  them plenty of sun. They need well-drained soil and
  water to their roots but usually not to their foliage.*

- *In colder climates, perennial herbs may naturally
  die down in the winter, aided by cutting back to the
  new growth at the base of the plant at this time.*

- *In warmer climates, regular pruning and a
  heavier annual cut back in winter may be
  required to maintain their dense, bushy shapes.*

- *Herbs generally need no more attention (feeding,
  pest and disease control) than other garden plants;
  very often they require less. Many are native to
  open and exposed places with poor soil and dry
  spells, so they can be surprisingly tough. They may
  even deteriorate if the conditions are too good.*

Index

A

Acer griseum 28
Acer palmatum 16
Acer palmatum
  'Atropurpureum' 13, 68
Acer palmatum 'Senkaki' 68
Acorus gramineus 95
African daisies 68
Agapanthus 26, 41
Ajuga reptans 16, 48
Alpine moss 105, 113
Annuals 34, 82
Aquilegias 48, 98
Arctotis 25, 68
Armeria maritima 71
Artemis 15, 127
Asplenium 27
Asplenium nidus 31
Avenues and copses of trees 33
Azaleas 51, 64, 79

B

Baby's tears 98
Backgrounds 89
Bark, making a feature of it 29
Begonias 83
Betula pendula 8, 33
Bird's nest ferns 31
Bluebells 64
Borage 69, 127
Borders, frames and 7
Boston ivy 56
Box 42
Box hedge 40, 41
Bromeliads 44
Building steps 75
Buxus microphylla 42
Buxus sempervirens 42

C

Camellias 52
Campanula 35, 82
Candytuft 64
Catmint 36, 126
Centranthus ruber 77
Cerastium tomentosum 81
Chinese cabbage 8
Chives 126
Choosing garden ornaments 97
Choosing plants for mass
  planting 26
Choosing plants for shady
  places 44
Choosing plants for your site 19
Chrysocoma 110
Cinerarias 8
Clematis 81
Clematis montana 'Elizabeth' 78
Climber for tree trunks 30
Climbers on houses, growing 79
Climbers to conceal structures ... 109
Climbing rose 90
Climbing rose 'Gold Bunny' 56
Coastal plants 18
Colour combinations 66
Colour schemes 65
Colour with annuals 82
Colour, meaning of 69
Combining colour 66
Combining herbs in the garden 125
Companion planting 123
Copses, avenues and 33
Coral tree 25
Corydalis lutea 47
Cotoneaster 120
Cotoneaster dammeri 16
Crassula 102
Crassula multicava 50
Creating a view 10
Creeping fig 121
Creeping thyme 126
Croweas 27
Ctenanthe 50
Cycads 119

D

Dahlias 83
Daisies 21, 26
Daisies, African 68
Daisies, Felicia 36
Daisies, shasta 34
Daisy bush 79
Decorative details 95
Delphiniums 97
Designing a formal garden 40
Dianthus .... 72 ,125
Duckweed 95
Dwarf box 110
Dwarf red maple 68

E

Easy care gardens 15
Echeveria 102
Elements of formal gardens 42
Elements that affect colour 68
English box 42
Enlarging small spaces 118
Epiphytes 30, 44
Erigeron 39, 82
Erigeron karvinskianus 81, 103
Erythrina x sykesii 25
Establishing plants in cracks 103
Eucalyptus citriodora 15
Evening primrose 79
Existing garden features,
  making use of 61

F

Felicia daisies 36
Fenceline flower planting 77
Ferns 119
Ficus pumila 121
Fleabane 81, 103
Flowering cherry 55
Flowering frontages 77
Flowers for shady places 51
Flowers in small spaces 34
Forget-me-nots 47, 51, 68, 69, 82
Formal gardens 39
Fountain 12
Foxgloves 11
Frames and borders 7
French marigolds 34
Fuchsias 52, 79
Fuss free gardening tips 21

G

Garden patterns 111
Garden pictures 95
Garden shed, transforming
  the 106
Garden treasures 61
Gardens with a view 5
Gazanias 18, 19, 82
Genista 67
Geranium robertianum 125
Geraniums 20, 34, 82, 9,3 97
Germander 42
Geum 66
Grass trees 27, 105
Grevilleas 27
Growing climbers on houses 79
Growing herbs successfully 127

H

Hedges 41, 42
Helichrysum petiolare
  'Aureum' 52
Herb garden 61, 125
Herb Robert 125
Herbal parterre 110
Herbs 57
Herbs, tips for success 127
Herbs, vegetables and 123
Hollyhocks 101
Honesty 48
Hosta 5, 48
Hottuynia cordata 'Variegata' 52
Hydrangeas 52

I, J

Iceplant 18
Impatiens 35
Iochroma cyaneum 98
Iris 25 26 82 97

Ivy 95
Ivy geraniums 21
Japanese box 42
Japanese maple 16 47
Japanese rose 53 93
Japanese sacred bamboo 96
Juniper 72
Juniperus conferta 72
Justicia 5

K

Kalanchoe 66
Kerria japonica 53, 93
Kitchen herb garden 61
Kniphofia uvaria 24

L

Laburnum 6, 7, 8
Lake, creating a 12
Lamb's ear 16
Laminum 47, 52, 98
Lamium maculatum 68
Lavender 15, 23, 39, 125, 126
Lavender cotton 57, 110
Lemon balm 125
Leopard plant 52
Ligularia tussilaginea 52
Lilies 48, 82
Linum 34
Lobelia 35, 83
Lupins 69, 101

M

Maidenhair fern 50
Maidenhair vine 30
Maple, paperbark 28
Maples 13
Marigolds 123
Marigolds, French 34
Mass planting 23
Melissa officinalis 125
Mentha spicata 125
Microclimates 63
Mondo grass 16, 42, 95, 103

N, O

Nandina domestica 96
Nigella 66
Ophiopogon japonicus 16, 103
Orchids 119
Oregano 126
Ornamental tobacco 79
Ornaments, use of in garden ... 11, 95
Osteospermum ecklonis 23

P

Pansies 35
Paperbark maple 28
Path edges 73
Path routes 72
Path surfaces 72
Paths and steps 71
Patterns in the garden 111
Pavilions, pergolas and 6
Pelargoniums 21, 35
Penstemon 83
Perennial wallflowers 26
Perennials 34
Perennials and climate 83
Pergolas and pavilions 6
Petunias 35, 36, 83
Pigface 18
Planning a small garden 120
Planting in crevices 102
Plants and stone 101
Plants in cracks, establishing 103
Pond, creating a 12
Pool, creating a 12

Poppies 127
Potatoes 124
Pretty compositions 95

R

Red hot pokers 24
Red valerian 77
Retaining walls 85
Rhododendrons 51
Romantic gardens 55
Rose 'Albertine' 77
Rose 'Bloomfield Courage' 108
Rose 'Gold Bunny' 56
Rose 'Iceberg' 36
Rosemary 126

S

Santolina chamaecyparissus 110
Sassafras 33
Scabious 82
Scleranthus biflorus 105, 113
Screens, walls and 85
Seasonal colour 34
Sedum 18, 102
Sempervivum 102
Shade, variations of 48
Shady places 44
Shasta daisies 34
Silver birches 8, 11, 33, 41
Simple structures 106
Single colour gardens 65
Small garden, tips for
  success 120
Small spaces 116, 118
Snow-in-summer 81
Spearmint 125
Spot colour (flowers) 34
Stachys byzantina 16
Starting a vegetable patch 124
Statice 18
Stepping stones 71
Steps, paths and 71
Steps, tips for building 75
Stone, use of in garden 101
Structures in the garden 106
Surfaces for paths 72
Sweet corn 124

T

Tansy .... 83 ,110
Thrift 71
Thyme .... 110 ,126
Tree ferns 27, 53, 119
Tree trunks 29
Trees with beautiful bark 29
Tulips 55

V

Vegetable patch, tips for
  success 124
Vegetables and herbs 123
Vinca minor 42
Violas 93
Violets 98
Viburnum plicatum 97

W

Walls and screens 85
Water features 12
Waterfall, creating a 12
Weeping fig 120
Windflowers 64
Woodland plants 5 9

X

Xanthorrhoea australis 105

CLIMATE ZONES

Our terms defined

COLD: Where average temperatures in winter are always below 0°C (32°F).
COOL: Where average temperatures in winter are between 0°-7°C (32°-45°F).
MILD: Where average temperatures in winter are above 7°C (45°F).
WARM: Where average temperatures in summer are below 20°C (68°F).
HOT: Where average temperatures in summer are above 20°C (68°F).